The Lead Docket Book

The Lead Docket Book

A Practical Guide to Boosting Intake Conversions and Better Tracking Your Marketing Efforts

Ivan Rodrigues

HOUNDSTOOTH
PRESS

THE LEAD DOCKET BOOK
A Practical Guide to Boosting Intake Conversions
and Better Tracking Your Marketing Efforts

FIRST EDITION

ISBN   978-1-5445-4995-8 *Hardcover*
   978-1-5445-4994-1 *Paperback*
   978-1-5445-4996-5 *Ebook*

Contents

Foreword

—Eric Coffman, Founder and Creator of Lead Docket

When I first began developing what would become Lead Docket, I wasn't trying to build a software company—I was simply trying to solve a painful, costly problem at the law firm where I was chief operating officer. We were losing leads. Not just a few here and there, but valuable opportunities were slipping through the cracks every week. I knew that if we didn't get a better handle on intake and follow-up, we'd continue to waste both time and revenue potential.

So I built a solution. Lead Docket was born out of necessity—designed specifically to ensure that every lead followed a defined, accountable path. It didn't take long to see the impact. By creating consistency in how leads were tracked, assigned, and followed up on, we didn't just stop the bleeding—we dramatically improved our efficiency and bottom line. The results were undeniable.

That same system now powers lead management for over

one thousand law firms, helping them achieve the same clarity, structure, and growth we experienced firsthand.

This book is an essential guide for getting the most out of Lead Docket. It captures not only the "how" but the "why"—why structured intake matters, why consistent follow-up converts, and why discipline in your process is the difference between stagnant growth and transformative results.

Whether you're just getting started or already using Lead Docket, I believe the principles in these pages will help your firm make smarter decisions, streamline your intake process, and capture the full value of every opportunity.

I'm proud to see this book published, and I'm honored to write this foreword. The tools are in your hands. Use them well.

Introduction

If you're reading this book, you likely fall into one of two categories: either you're considering buying Lead Docket, or you're already a user, perhaps pondering how to maximize its capabilities. In either case, your journey with Lead Docket can be likened to that of owning a really powerful car. Let's call it a Ferrari. (I'm not exactly a car person, but that sounds right...)

Just like a Ferrari, Lead Docket is a top-of-its-field solution, built upon sophisticated technology and designed for high performance. (Now I am committed to this metaphor, so bear with me...) Whether you're a potential buyer stepping into the showroom or an existing owner sitting in the driver's seat, the question remains the same: "How can I tap into the full potential of this powerful machine?"

In my years of experience, as both a user and a consultant for various Lead Docket clients, I've observed a common scenario: many Ferrari owners, so to speak, rarely shift beyond the first gear. They possess this performance powerhouse, yet they barely scratch the surface of what it can do. They either haven't been shown how to utilize its full potential, or they don't even realize the power that's available to them.

This book is intended to bridge that gap. It's designed to guide you, whether you're just getting acquainted with Lead Docket or seeking to deepen your existing knowledge. The aim is not to overwhelm you with information but to provide practical, manageable steps to help you harness the full power of your Ferrari. (Ok, I think I'm done with this metaphor for now...)

Think of this as a journey toward becoming a more effective manager of your Lead Docket. It's about learning to navigate or at least make a conscious decision to use (or not use) its advanced features and capabilities. By the end of this book, you should be more confident in your ability to leverage this powerful tool, pushing it beyond the basics and into the realm of true expertise.

BEFORE WE BEGIN: WHO AM I?

Not long ago, I was exactly where you are now. For several years, I served as the marketing and intake director at a midsize personal injury law firm in Tennessee. That role introduced me to Lead Docket, where we had nine intake agents and two marketing staff actively working with the platform.

My experience began purely as a user—I rolled up my sleeves, dug into every feature, and probably drove the Lead Docket support team a little crazy. But eventually, we took off with the tool, and let me tell you, the feeling of watching a system propel your firm to the next level is exhilarating.

Today, I have the privilege of helping dozens of firms navigate that same exciting journey. My goal with this book is straightforward: to deliver practical value quickly, whether you're a firm owner, intake manager, or part of the intake staff. Beyond technical instructions, you'll find valuable business insights here: essential key performance indicators (KPIs) to track, important questions your intake team should be asking, and tips for handling the challenges of change management.

Throughout this book, you'll notice various QR codes. Scan them to access video recordings that expand upon the chapter's content. These videos aren't just helpful for visual learners—they're also yours to integrate into your team's training resources.

SO, WHAT IS LEAD DOCKET AGAIN?

Have you ever found yourself pondering, even after purchasing or using Lead Docket for a while, "What exactly does this tool do?" Well, you're not alone. So, before we dive in, let's clarify that very question. Even if you think you're familiar with it, the upcoming paragraphs might just reveal some features you had no idea existed.

Key features of Lead Docket:

1. Lead capture: This isn't just about gathering leads from different sources like websites, web chats, and answering services. It's also about seamless integration with tools like CallRail and Call Tracking Metrics to automatically pinpoint where each lead came from with tons of metadata like campaign info, keyworks, call transcripts, Urchin Tracking Module (UTM) codes, etc. Lead Docket acts as a hub collecting leads from all possible sources.
2. Customizable workflows: Tailor the lead management process to fit the unique needs and preferences of your firm. This means creating statuses and steps to move prospective clients into signed clients. It's like having a suit custom-made for your business's specific requirements.
3. Referral tracking: Automate messages and follow-ups with

referral partners so you can track every referred-out case meticulously. It also gives referral partners a login-free dashboard to manage the leads they received from you and to give you updates.

4. Automated follow-ups: Say goodbye to missed opportunities with automated emails and texts sent to leads. And the best part? Every aspect of these messages is customizable and trackable.

5. Task management: Automate the distribution of tasks to your team, tailored to each lead's needs. Create and assign tasks to ensure that no lead falls through the cracks. One of Lead Docket's most powerful impacts is that no lead is left untouched. That alone moves the conversion needle.

6. Document management: Keep all your lead-related documents organized and easily transferable to your case management software. Use a short message service (SMS) to easily gather docs and send Vinesign contracts in a few clicks while you have the lead on the phone.

7. Communication tracking: Maintain a comprehensive record of all communications with leads, including emails, phone calls, and texts. This ensures that a clear history of interactions is always at your fingertips.

8. Reporting and analytics: Arm yourself with detailed reports on lead conversion rates, team performance, and other crucial metrics. This feature is all about making informed, data-driven decisions.

9. AI analysis: Take advantage of industry tailored and carefully designed AI prompts to summarize leads and messages and even predict the likelihood of a fee.

10. Payments: Receive payments right into Lead Docket with an easy-to-use platform.

While this list isn't exhaustive, it covers the broad strokes of what Lead Docket is capable of. Within each of these areas lies a treasure trove of tools that, when configured correctly, can eliminate manual errors and streamline your use of Lead Docket.

Given that Lead Docket is a dynamic, ever-evolving software, and this book is a static medium, we'll strive to update this content regularly to reflect the latest features. For the most current information, you can always check out the Lead Docket website (https://www.leaddocket.com/).

Chapter 01

Unboxing a Brand-New Lead Docket

This section is especially tailored for those who have just joined the Lead Docket family. If you're a seasoned user, feel free to skip this part. Chances are you've already navigated through the hurdles we're about to discuss, that hopefully this book will help new users avoid. If you have faced some hiccups in your implementation, you most likely suffer from "bad implementation" side effects. This chapter will help you identify what may have gone wrong.

First off, congratulations on acquiring Lead Docket! You probably went through one or more impressive sales demos, but now it's time to actually see it working for your firm. The promise of cutting-edge legal tech delivering results comes down to using it well as a team. You took the first step! Now what?

If you were to receive the login to your brand new Lead Docket, you'll find a blank canvas. You'll need an implementation partner to get the system up and running. Filevine has a number of certified implementation partners that can assist you in this process. You may even be introduced to one by your Filevine salesperson, but you can find all the options here: https://www.filevine.com/partners/directory/.

I would encourage you to ask for more than one quote, but don't stop at the quote. A thirty-minute discovery call is well worth the years of system use, and it can save you from future headaches. Always stay in touch with your Filevine account manager to provide feedback on the partner services you receive. That feedback is taken very seriously at Filevine and helps our whole community grow.

Now, as you start to hear what the implementation will look like, keep this in mind: the setup process varies greatly. While some may claim it's a one-size-fits-all solution, the reality is far from it.

Having personally implemented dozens of Lead Docket systems for a wide range of firms, from solo practitioners to organizations with hundreds of staff, I can assure you *that a meticulous and successful setup is crucial for making the most of Lead Docket.* Let's dive into some of the essential configurations required during the implementation phase and highlight a few common pitfalls that are often encountered in the implementation process.

LEAD DOCKET FOR NONPERSONAL INJURY PRACTICES

Straight out of the gate, it's important to recognize that Lead Docket (at the time of writing this book in mid-2025) was primarily crafted with personal injury firms in mind. Its default statuses, message templates, and task workflows are inherently designed to cater to the needs of its largest user base—personal injury practitioners. However, if your practice lies outside the realm of personal injury law (say, in fields like immigration or employment law, and even real estate), you'll want to pay extra attention to the default configurations of the tool, which are often overlooked during the setup phase.

For nonpersonal injury practices, the implementation journey is a bit more intricate due to the distinctive nature of your processes. It's crucial for your implementation consultant to gain a deep understanding of your intake steps in order to accurately replicate them using Lead Docket's customizable statuses and workflows.

One of Lead Docket's standout features is its ability to tailor statuses and substatuses, lending incredible flexibility to the system. However, this same versatility can lead to unnecessary complexity if the transition between each status isn't meticulously planned out. For practices outside the personal injury sphere, this means a more hands-on, detailed approach to configuring Lead Docket to ensure that it perfectly aligns with your firm's unique workflow needs.

Chapter 01.01

The Big Picture

Embarking on the journey of setting up Lead Docket from scratch is no small feat. Here, we present a comprehensive list of tasks that typically form the backbone of a basic implementation. Keep in mind that these tasks may vary based on the size of your firm and your specific practice areas. While the list may seem daunting at first glance, rest assured that many of these tasks are straightforward. *The length of the list is a testament to the thoroughness required, not the difficulty.* Consider this your road map or checklist, whether you're spearheading the implementation yourself or working alongside an implementation partner.

In the following sections, we'll delve into some of these tasks in greater detail, while others will receive a more concise overview. Our goal is to direct you to valuable resources for the more intricate features and ensure that you have a clear understanding of the full array of features and functionalities that Lead Docket offers. This chapter is designed to provide you with a bird's-eye view of the setup process, equipping you with the knowledge to navigate through the intricacies of Lead Docket.

BASIC SYSTEM SETUP

General settings

Update options

Upload logo and change colors

Add all case types

Confirm Filevine and Vinesign connected

Add offices

Upload/add users

Register for phone service (A2P)

Intake and Mapping

Connect case types to Filevine Templates

Add custom fields/intake

Map native fields

Add custom contact card questions and map

Map users to Filevine

Update marketing and contact sources

Update phase mapping

Test lead pushed to Filevine

Messages and Tasks

Review task templates

Review message templates

Set up document templates

Set up lead forms

ADVANCED SETTINGS

System Integrations

Connect Docusign/Vinesign

Connect CallRail/CTM (if applicable, but encouraged)

Create Webhooks for all lead sources

Other

Upload/add referral sources

Add texting number

Role mapping to Filevine

Upload Vinesign templates

Import expenses spreadsheet

Enable auto replies to opportunities

Confirm integrations completed

Add message snippets

Add-ons

Set up automation rules (if applicable)

Data migration

AI fields

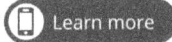

Online version of the checklist can be found here.

Chapter 01.02

Basic Setup

Alright, you've officially unboxed your shiny new Lead Docket environment, and it's ready for customization. The first tasks you'll tackle are the basic system settings. Think of this step as setting your mirrors and adjusting your seat to make sure your drive is comfortable and efficient.

UPDATE OPTIONS UNDER SETTINGS TO TAILOR TO YOUR NEEDS

Head over to Manage > Settings > Options. This is your opportunity to fine-tune Lead Docket exactly to your preferences:

- **Enable simplified settlement entry:** Simplifies the settlement screen to focus only on fees, ideal if detailed settlement information isn't required.
- **Allow referring directly to "Signed Up" status:** This setting has to be used with care. It opens up room for manual errors. The only reason to use it is if the firm taking the call is actually signing the lead on behalf of the referral partner.

In that case, it allows leads to be directly referred to "Signed Up" without having to go through a pending review.

- **Show default role selection on change status screen:** Displays "Assign to Intake" when updating a lead's status, streamlining user interactions.
- **Enable contact timezone:** Automatically assigns a timezone based on contact details, essential for managing communications across regions.
- **Enable Filevine phase mapping/end notes and messages to Filevine:** Crucial for ensuring seamless integration, automatically syncing notes and messages directly to Filevine.

These seemingly small decisions can significantly impact your team's workflow, so don't overlook them!

UPLOAD YOUR LOGO AND SET UP YOUR BRAND COLOR

Make Lead Docket your own by uploading your firm's logo and customizing colors. Navigate to Manage > Settings > Logo. A consistent visual identity helps your team feel comfortable and connected with the tool from day one.

CONFIRM THAT FILEVINE AND VINESIGN ARE CONNECTED

Ensure seamless connectivity:

- **Filevine Integration:** Confirm your leads are correctly mapped and flowing smoothly from Lead Docket into Filevine templates. This is usually done by the Filevine team.
- **Vinesign Integration:** Run a test to make sure document

signing and management work flawlessly. This quick check prevents future headaches.

ADD OFFICES TO LEAD DOCKET

If your firm has multiple offices, adding them is a good idea. Go to Manage > Offices and list each location. Doing this correctly enhances your reporting capabilities, lets you track office-specific marketing efforts, and ensures accuracy on automated messages.

Offices is also a field that we often use for other purposes. Think of it as a card up your sleeve when you need triggers and criteria to filter reports and automations. (If you aren't sure what this means, don't worry. We'll cover that later.)

Ok, you are all set on your basic settings. Let's move on.

Chapter 01.03

User Settings

Once you've nailed down the basic settings, personalized your logo, and perhaps added your brand colors, it's time to focus on providing access to other users within Lead Docket.

It's essential to remember the distinction between licensed and unlicensed users. You might have come across this during the sales process. To put it simply:

- **Licensed Users:** These are the individuals who have the ability to log in and interact with your Lead Docket system. Typically, they are the ones handling intake, running reports, and navigating the system. It's worth noting that even for licensed users, you can restrict access to specific sections of the software on an individual basis.
- **Unlicensed Users:** This category is for those who can be assigned to a lead in Lead Docket but don't have the capability to log in or make changes. This setup is ideal for attorneys who may not need direct access to Lead Docket but still need to be kept in the loop about certain leads. Unlicensed users can receive notifications, calendar invites, and email messages, and their responses are all tracked within Lead Docket.

When setting up user accounts, keeping the above distinction in mind is crucial. Additionally, there are several key steps to follow for a seamless setup:

Add User

First Name	
Last Name	
Initials	
Email	
Username	
New Password	
Phone Number	
Default Texting Number	-- Choose Default Number --
Default Outbound Caller ID Number	-- Choose Default Number --
Default Office	-- Choose Default Office --
Time Zone	-- Select Timezone --
Filevine Contact Id	
Filevine User Id	
Email Calendar Invites To	Semicolon separated list of email addresses (Optional)
Message Notification	☐ Send email notifications when messages are received on assigned leads.
Active?	☑ Can be associated with leads and receive emails.
Licensed	☑ Can login and manage leads.

Browse ↑

Browse ↑

- Filevine Integration: For Filevine users, make sure to add their Filevine contact ID and user ID by using the browse feature. This ensures that their information syncs correctly with Filevine.
- Email and Calendar Invites: Input their emails in the "Email Calendar Invites To" field. This step is vital to ensure they receive calendar invites for scheduled appointments.
- Direct Phone Numbers: Including their direct phone numbers allows you to utilize the phone call feature within Lead Docket effectively. (More on this later.)
- Assigning Roles: Ensure each user is assigned the appropriate role. This is done by selecting the relevant checkboxes that align with their functions within your firm.
- Setting Permissions: Assign the correct permissions that correspond to their role. This is crucial for maintaining the integrity and security of your system.

In summary, setting up users in Lead Docket is about more than just adding names; it's about customizing their experience and access to fit their role and the needs of your firm.

One final note—for larger firms, this can be done in bulk by importing a spreadsheet under Manage > Import. All the same characteristics will apply.

Chapter 01.04

Customizing Your Statuses

For many years, Lead Docket had just eleven fixed statuses. Then came customizable statuses, opening the door to creative work-flows—especially for nonpersonal injury firms. Now, the ability to customize might feel exciting, but proceed carefully: just because you can do something doesn't always mean you should. Excessive customizations can quickly turn your sleek sports car into Frankenstein's minivan, especially if you're tempted to replicate your legacy system. For most personal injury or contingency-based firms, Lead Docket's out-of-the-box statuses cover nearly everything you'll need. They're intentionally designed, carefully tested, and generally play nicely with other features.

Think of statuses as conveyor belts on an assembly line. Each lead moves smoothly from creation toward a terminal status—typically "signed," "lost," or "rejected." These are the finish lines for your leads. Active statuses, meanwhile, are more like waiting rooms: think Chase, Scheduled, Hold, or Under Review. These represent leads that have life left in them.

Here's a quick rundown of the essential statuses to get familiar with.

SIGNED UP

Lead Docket allows only one "Signed Up" status, and there's a good reason for this: it tracks your official count of signed cases by the date the lead moves into this status. If you shuffle signed leads into another status—even temporarily—they vanish from your signed lead counts. The bottom line: if there's a contract signed, keep that lead firmly in "Signed Up."

CLOSED

"Closed" in Lead Docket isn't just another inactive bucket—it means the lead was signed, handled, settled, and officially wrapped up. You can't delete or repurpose this status. That said, reality can get messy—cases stall, clients switch attorneys, or attorneys drop cases. To keep things tidy, create clear substatuses under "Closed" like "Settled," "Dropped," or even the candid but honest "Client Fired Us." Avoid moving closed leads to "Lost" or "Rejected," or you might find yourself wondering why last year's signed leads suddenly disappeared.

CHASE

An effective strategy we've seen is splitting your Chase leads into two buckets. Bucket One holds Chase leads you've confirmed as Wanted/Qualified, while Bucket Two contains those you haven't managed to speak with yet. Trust me, your future reports and conversion tracking will thank you for clearly separating these leads (more on this later).

Here is a walkthrough of how Chase statuses are designed in Lead Docket.

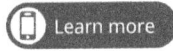

REFERRED OUT

Be cautious about customizing the "Referred Out" substatuses. They're intentionally structured to work smoothly with Lead Docket's referral dashboard, and too many changes can break that smooth operation.

One small "hack" you may not know is that you can add one more substatus on the referral dashboard for partner firms. One interesting use, for example, is creating a "Dropped" substatus to distinguish between leads your partners declined outright and those they initially signed but later released. Additionally, creating internal-only substatuses like "Referred—Archived" helps keep things neat behind the scenes without cluttering the partner's view.

In short, customizing statuses is powerful, but wield that power wisely. A thoughtful balance between creativity and practicality ensures your Lead Docket stays finely tuned.

USING "SUBSTATUS REASONS"

It's also worth mentioning that Lead Docket has substatuses for each status that are helpful ways to break down, for example, reasons for a rejected lead. But what many people don't know is that Lead Docket also has something called Substatus Reasons. It works effectively as sub-substatuses.

They are specially helpful in the Referred Out status since you do not want to add many substatuses there and break the referral dashboard. Substatus Reasons are very versatile, and I've seen them used in many different ways. To enable, go to Manage > Statuses, click the Status you want, navigate to the Substatus, and click Edit. You'll see this side panel:

Chapter 01.05

Adding Case Types

Calling this step "simple" is like calling IKEA instructions "straightforward"—technically true, but highly debatable.

So, we've dedicated a chapter to adding case types. Although it may seem like just a list of practice areas, it actually determines a significant part of the workflow in Lead Docket.

This is something that an implementation partner may overlook because it's technically simple but can impact your processes for years to come.

Here are a few considerations to keep in mind before you build this list:

- Each case type can be mapped to one Filevine template. Multiple Lead Docket case types can push to the same Filevine project type.
- Case types are required fields and used as filters for messages, tasks, and automations. They are also easily reported on.
- Your intake questions will be built by case type, meaning that fields will appear or not depending on the case type. You can also do this using a secondary field, but you'll have limitations.

In practical terms, there are two ways you can build your case types: broad categories and specific case types.

Broad categories: Here, you would have, for example, personal injury as a case type, and you would create a custom field called Subtype to track: MVA, commercial, pedestrian, dog bite, slip and fall, etc. Another example is creating a mass tort case type and a field with all the subtypes of mass torts your firm practices.

Pros: This could make the selection of case type during an intake much easier if you have dozens of mass torts or PI categories. We've seen the case type list get really long.

Cons: This makes reporting harder and since your subtype field is not available on message templates, tasks, etc. This also makes it more difficult to tailor those.

We would generally not recommend this approach.

Specific case types: You should be able to create case types for specific practices without too much trouble. In this scenario, you would create one case type for each (MVA, commercial MVA, pedestrian, dog bite, etc.). You would similarly break down your mass torts in their own case type, such as RoundUp, hernia mesh, 3M, etc.

Pros: This makes it easy to report on and tailor your messages.

Con: It can make building your intake questions a little harder since questions will show in multiple case types.

As long as you don't get too granular and break down dozens of practice areas, this approach should work well. It's usually what we recommend.

Pro tip 1: Unrelated Practice Area: by default, Lead Docket offers this case type so you can capture leads from areas that your firm doesn't practice, but don't overlook this! The information captured here has made thousands of dollars for one of the firms we worked with. They realized that they were getting many family law leads and created a lucrative referral program. Keep an eye on these!

Pro tip 2: Remove "Other" from your case types. You want your intake team to use "Unrelated Practice Area" as much as possible since that case type has a required field that pops · up asking for the practice area.

Chapter 01.06

Intake Questions

Now that you have case types set up, it's time for one of the most important parts of your Lead Docket build: building your intake questionnaire.

In this part, you will be setting up the questions that will guide the flow of the intake call. You should keep several factors in mind as you design this questionnaire:

- The user experience from your lead perspective: when you call your cable company, how do you like that call to be handled? Doesn't it bother you when they ask for all your contact information before asking what you're calling about? Remember that you definitely need some basic information to be captured right away, but keep the end user in mind as you design the intake script.
- The user experience of your intake agent: how many clicks and buttons do they have to press, and how much are they scrolling, all while trying to be empathetic and listen to your lead?
- What are your qualifying questions that need to be answered

right away before you go deeper into the details? What questions could be gathered at a later time or even using a lead form feature that allows the lead to answer at their own time?

- Can you guide your intake person through this process using instruction text and prompts?

If you're setting up Lead Docket for the first time, take this opportunity to revise and revamp your current intake process. You may have been doing something for years in a different system. Moving to a new system allows the opportunity to review what's working and to improve any flaws or obstacles. A good implementation partner should be able to advise you on the best practices around your questionnaire.

In a nutshell, your questionnaire will consist of custom fields that you will build under Manage > Custom Fields.

FIELD TYPES

Pay special attention to the field types you use. We see many instances of firms using text fields to capture things like "insurance company" or "treatment status." Keep the data integrity and ease of reporting in mind when you build these. Text fields can be great now, but they might give you data nightmares in the future. Think of your reporting and the case management system you will push that info into.

On the other hand, a slightly more complex issue is that using Filevine's contact fields can also create issues with duplicate contacts in Filevine. So be mindful of that and discuss the pros and cons with your implementation partner.

IMPORTING YOUR INTAKE QUESTIONS (IN CASE YOU USE FILEVINE)

Your implementation partner should have access to a tool that allows you to import intake questions directly from your Filevine. This is extremely helpful if you have spent time and energy building your Filevine intake. But it can also be a trap if you have a poorly built intake in Filevine and will now have a poorly built intake in Lead Docket. Take this time to improve it!

FILEVINE MAPPING

After finishing your questions, you will want to map them to the proper field in Filevine. (If you have imported them, they will come in mapped!) This step is important because some of the default fields in Lead Docket will have to be mapped. For instance, the intake person who handled the intake, the sign-up date, and the lead created date can all be mapped.

Pro tip: Create a field in Filevine to house your Lead ID and map it there. This is super simple, and we highly recommend it. It can save you many headaches in the future.

USING REQUIRED FIELDS

Something to keep in mind is that you can set up fields to be required at a certain status. This is a huge help in maintaining the integrity of your data. Check out the video below for more details on how to do it. We'll explain more and share some common use cases in Chapter 3.

SCAN ME

Learn more

Status Required Fields—four minutes

DESIGN IDEAS

As you add fields, you'll need to order and adjust their width. Keep in mind some basic design principles. Try to align fields as much as possible. Use underlined characters to create lines and separate your sections. Here are some examples:

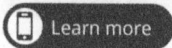

☆ Add Lead

Were there any witnesses?

○ Yes ● No ○ Unknown

Were there any other passengers in the vehicle?

● Yes ○ No ○ Unknown

ⓘ Additional passengers should be added as related contacts in the top right corner.

Brief Insurance Information

Initial Insurance Notes

Does the Lead have insurance?

○ Yes ○ No ● Unknown

Does the Defendant has insurance?

○ Yes ○ No ● Unknown

Injury Details

Describe Injuries

Initial Treatment

☐ Ambulance
☐ Hospital
☐ Urgent Care
☐ Other

Permanent Injury?

○ Yes ○ No ● Unknown

Using bars and headings

☆ Add Lead

Defendant's Vehicle Details

Defendant's Vehicle - Year, Make & Model   Defendant's License Plate State & No.   Defendant's Vehicle VIN

Damage to Defendant's Vehicle   Defendant's Vehicle Towed

--Choose--   Yes   No   ⦿ Unknown

Wrap Up

Please select applicable items that have   Additional Info
been received

◻ Client Completed Online Intake Form
◻ Health Insurance Card Copies (Front & Back)
◻ Injury Photos
◻ Property Damage Photos
◻ Signed Welcome Letter w/ Retainer &
  Authorizations

Severity Level *   Office * (Client: CA)   Assigned To Intake agent *

-- Choose Severity Level --   -- Choose Office --   Ivan Rodrigues

Lead Status *

-- Choose Status --

Using instruction text and conditional fields

Chapter 01.07

Marketing Fields

Later in this book, there will be an entire chapter dedicated specifically to tracking your marketing efforts in Lead Docket. It's a common question we frequently hear from both new firms and those who've been using Lead Docket for years. Clearly defining your Marketing Source and your Contact Source is crucial for generating reliable reports and insightful analytics in the long run. Check out that chapter for an in-depth exploration of the best practices for marketing tracking within Lead Docket.

For now, as you're setting up your new Lead Docket environment, there are two key points you should keep in mind:

1. The **Marketing Source** is always required. So is a **Contact Source**—but here's a little-known trick: you can actually remove the Contact Source field entirely if it doesn't fit your workflow.
2. Another key piece of marketing data is the **Referred By** field. Here's how it works: whenever "Referral" is chosen as your Marketing Source, your intake agent must indicate who referred that lead. Although agents can type freely, we

strongly recommend using the search feature and selecting a predefined referral source. Yes, it requires a bit more upfront work (under Manage > Referral Sources), but trust me, the improved reporting is absolutely worth the effort as it ensures more accurate reporting down the line. This is especially helpful if your firm tracks who referred cases and maybe pays a fee back to those sources. Then you truly want to make sure the intake person selects the source, instead of free typing it.

It's helpful to have a crystal clear definition of what a Marketing Source and a Contact Source is. I can't stress this enough. We work with several firms who started with a blurry definition and now we have to clean up dozens of misplaced sources that don't make sense anymore. Lead Docket's intended definitions are:

- **Marketing Source:** How the person found out about you—typically via some paid advertising medium such as TV, Google, a referral relationship, etc.
- **Contact Source:** How they contacted you—web chat, web form, call, etc.

(Sometimes they can be the same, but, for example, web chat is squarely NOT a Marketing Source. It's a clear Contact Source.)

We at Vineskills have put together a "template" of how we suggest firms use these fields. It has helped many firms, so we decided to make it available for you here.

Scan this code to get a list of sources:

SCAN ME

Learn more

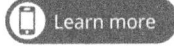

The question often arises: "Can I move the marketing information box to the bottom of my intake?" The answer is no. And if this makes you mad and seems like a big deal, just take a deep breath. Once you start using it, it won't be.

Pro Tip: You can add a brief description or instruction to help your intake team ask the right questions—see this screenshot:

Marketing Information

ℹ You can add instruction text here if you'd like

Marketing Source * ℹ	Contact Source * ℹ	Marketing Source Details	Referred By	Search
--Choose Source--	--Choose Source--			

Chapter 01.08

Message Templates

Message templates in Lead Docket are designed to simplify and standardize your communication process. They are designed to send email and SMS to leads and referral partners, not to send employees information. Rather than reinventing messages for every interaction, templates provide your intake team with a reliable starting point. Lead Docket comes with pre-built message templates, but they're intentionally generic. You'll want to review and customize them to reflect your firm's voice and specific workflow.

HOW TO SET UP MESSAGE TEMPLATES

Navigate to Manage > Message Templates:

- **Create Template:** Choose the format (email or text), define the specific statuses to trigger the message, and give your template a clear, descriptive title.
- **Variables and Placeholders:** Use placeholders such as {ContactName}, {LeadId}, or {ContactEmail} to personal-

ize messages automatically. These can make your messages sound real and personal. Be careful with overusing it, though. You need to ensure the field is filled out, or the message will show up blank.

- **Attachments and Links:** Easily include documents or links (we have seen a lot of success with YouTube links and even some small pictures). Avoid large attachments, as some phone carriers may block them.

CREATION RULES AND TRIGGERS

- **Creation Rules:** Define conditions under which a specific message template automatically triggers. For example, set rules that automatically send a message when a lead status changes to "Chase" or "Pending Sign-up."
- **Triggers:** Triggers activate messages based on events like status changes or specific actions within Lead Docket. These can be confusing. One quick tip is to duplicate other messages instead of creating new ones so the triggers will be the same. It took me months of bothering my colleague Shadae to double-check them until I finally understood them.

IMPORTANT CONSIDERATIONS

- **Chase and Pending Sign-up:** Pay special attention to messages for statuses like "Chase" and "Pending Sign-up." These stages often determine lead conversion and need thoughtfully crafted messages.

RECOMMENDED BEST PRACTICES

- Regularly review your templates for accuracy, relevancy, and tone.
- Keep your messages concise, friendly, and professional. Avoid overly complicated or lengthy messages.
- Regularly update your templates based on feedback from your intake team to ensure continuous improvement.

Pro Tip 1: We suggest testing different languages and approaches to these messages. Consider running a one-month test with a certain tone or format, then evaluate results to find what resonates best with your leads.

Pro Tip 2: Use Message Snippets! These are huge time savers for your intake agent. Find out more here:

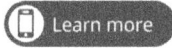

How to Configure and Use Message Snippets—four minutes

Chapter 01.09

Task Templates

Tasks in Lead Docket help ensure nothing slips through the cracks. They allow your team to manage responsibilities clearly and efficiently, making sure that each lead receives appropriate and timely attention throughout the intake process. They are usually automated through "templates" but can also be created manually.

Tasks guide the lead management process by prompting specific actions, such as making calls, sending follow-up communications, or collecting important documents. They are designed to be sent to your team, not to leads or referral partners, and are usually shown inside Lead Docket. The user can also receive them via email.

Be careful not to overbuild here. One of the main adoption issues we see arise from "too many" or unnecessary tasks that overwhelm the intake agents, and they stop using it altogether.

CREATING A TASK TEMPLATE

Navigate to Manage > Task Templates:

1. Click "Create New Task Template."
2. Name your template to reflect the task action, e.g., "Initial Follow-up Call."
3. Choose conditions that will trigger the task—such as status updates, only on specific case types, or certain severity levels.
4. Set task timing: due immediately or after a specified period like days or hours after triggering.
5. Assign responsibility—decide whether the task goes to a specific user or role.

VIEWING YOUR AND YOUR TEAM'S UNRESOLVED TASKS

To manage your ongoing responsibilities effectively:

- Go to the "Tasks" tab on your Lead Docket main navigation.
- Select "My Tasks" to see your unresolved tasks or "Team Tasks" to view unresolved tasks assigned across your entire team.
- Use the provided filters to sort tasks by due date, responsible team member, or task type.

RECOMMENDED USES FOR TASK

- **Immediate Follow-ups:** Tasks to prompt a quick follow-up call or email after a new lead submission.
- **Chase and Pending Sign-up:** Set tasks for timely follow-ups on leads that haven't yet signed a retainer.
- **Document Collection:** Tasks reminding your intake team to gather specific documents or details needed for case initiation.
- **Automated Notifications:** You can automatically send

notifications through tasks—even notifying attorneys of upcoming consultations directly via email.

IMPORTANT CONSIDERATIONS

- Tasks can automatically trigger email notifications, keeping team members informed without manual intervention. For example, notifying attorneys about scheduled consultations can be handled effortlessly with automated tasks.
- Even unlicensed users can receive task notifications, keeping your entire team informed and coordinated.

BEST PRACTICES

- Regularly check your unresolved tasks and address overdue items promptly.
- Monitor task completion to ensure workload balance among team members.
- Update task templates based on team feedback and performance observations.

Pro tip: Review your team's unresolved task list weekly. If there are tasks that are not getting done, consider disabling those task templates. Adjust them as needed based on how your team interacts with tasks, removing any that are redundant and enhancing those that improve productivity and workflow.

Chapter 02

Optimizing Your Lead Docket

This section is crafted for firms at various stages of using Lead Docket. Whether you've been utilizing it for an extended period with a large team or you're fresh off the implementation phase and curious about its full range of capabilities, this chapter is for you. It's crucial to understand that initial implementations, or as we've started to refer to them, "launches," only scratch the surface of what Lead Docket can do. Think of it as the beginning of the journey of using, testing, and enhancing your Lead Docket experience. This chapter is dedicated to that continuous improvement.

In our consulting work with Lead Docket and Filevine users, we often emphasize the concept of "optimizing," which is intertwined with the business philosophy of continuous improvement. This is vital for keeping your firm ahead of the curve. A reality check we often share with our clients (and that they don't always like to hear) is that the systems driving your firm need ongoing attention to stay current and efficient. This means that your initial investment in Lead Docket is just the beginning. Continuous investment, be it in financial resources or staff time, is essential for maintaining optimal performance of your systems.

But here's the encouraging part: in the realm of technology, even minor upgrades can lead to significant operational improvements. IT and tech professionals are like diamond hunters seeking ways to enhance your processes. One single find can potentially save substantial time and money. I've worked with firms who, within the first month or two of optimization, reduced intake call duration by half, significantly increased conversions, and in one case, automated five hours of weekly work for a manager down to mere seconds. Later in this chapter, we'll explore some of these transformative case studies.

We will start with the marketing capabilities of Lead Docket, then transition into the features related to intake management.

Chapter 02.01

Tracking Your Marketing Efforts

One of the greatest benefits Lead Docket brings to your firm is the ability to track and improve the return on investment of your marketing spend. To do this, we need as much detailed metadata from your lead sources as possible. As you expand your marketing efforts, always remember this golden rule: every source of leads should be integrated into Lead Docket with as much metadata as possible.

Unfortunately, this critical step is often overlooked during the implementation phase. Many consultants integrate sources into Lead Docket with only minimal required data. As a result, when you see an opportunity appear from a source like Google Ads, you might only see basic details such as the client's name and phone number. You're missing out on valuable insights, like campaign names, keywords, UTM codes, and even the Google Click ID—data that can significantly improve your conversion rate when utilized properly.

If terms like "UTM codes" or "Google Click ID" sound confusing, don't worry—you don't need to become an expert on marketing attribution. But a basic understanding will ensure you're equipped to ask your marketing vendor or systems admin to set up your integrations correctly.

Before we dive into how to set up your sources to properly track data, it is important to note that the top-level attribution starts with your Marketing Source and Contact Source fields. They are the key to most reporting and 80 percent of your insights will come from them (if properly set up). So take a look at your list right now. If it's messy and confusing, don't despair. Go back to Chapter 1.07 "Marketing Fields" and make sure to read the definitions and recommendations. Cleaning these sources is well worth the effort. Do it sooner rather than later.

REVIEWING AND SETTING UP INTEGRATIONS

To get started, go to Manage > Integrations in Lead Docket. Here you'll see a list of your lead sources, and when you click on each source, you can view all the fields you're currently receiving. Lead Docket has several marketing-related fields available by default, and you should aim to have all these fields integrated for each source:

- Campaign
- Keywords
- UTM codes
- Referring URL
- Current URL
- Click ID
- Client ID

CALL TRACKING

Tracking your digital marketing efforts is important, but for many law firms, a significant number of leads come from phone calls. Simply put, you should strongly consider using call tracking software like CallRail or Call Tracking Metrics if you spend money on marketing. (Note: I'm not affiliated with these systems, but I've seen firsthand the value firms gain from using call tracking software.)

Call tracking software allows you to create unique, trackable phone numbers that route directly to your main line. For example, you might create specific numbers for your website, billboards, TV ads, or various Google Ads campaigns. Each call to these numbers is tracked, allowing you to easily see which marketing sources are most effective. Moreover, these tools also work effectively with pay-per-click campaigns (e.g., Google Ads, social media ads) and track the same critical metadata mentioned earlier.

Both CallRail and Call Tracking Metrics integrate natively with Lead Docket, making setup straightforward. Navigate to Settings > Integrations in Lead Docket to configure your call tracking software.

Pro tip: If you have set up complex attribution rules in Lead Docket, keep in mind that phone calls typically override other source rules. (If this sounds confusing, don't worry—we'll clarify this further in the upcoming chapters.)

Chapter 02.02

Attribution Models (Let's Get Nerdy for a Second)

Let's take a moment to understand why collecting all this metadata is important by diving into the concept of marketing attribution. Attribution models are to marketers what *Game of Thrones* characters are to TV viewers: overly complicated but somehow necessary.

There are extensive materials and countless classes dedicated to attribution models, so don't worry—you don't need to become an expert. Instead, let's focus on understanding some key concepts.

UNDERSTANDING ATTRIBUTION MODELS

There are many attribution models used to track the effectiveness of marketing campaigns. The most common models include:

- **First-Touch Attribution:** This model gives credit to the first marketing interaction a lead had with your firm. For example, if a client sees your TV ad, then searches online and clicks on your Google Ads, first-touch attribution credits the TV ad for attracting the lead.
- **Last-Touch Attribution:** This model assigns credit to the last marketing interaction before a lead takes action. Using the same scenario, the Google Ads click would receive credit since it was the last interaction before the lead submitted a form. Lead Docket primarily operates on a last-touch attribution model, which is usually the most effective for law firms.
- **Multi-Touch Attribution:** This model distributes credit across multiple touchpoints along a client's journey. Although some firms experiment with multi-touch or weighted attributions by creating custom fields or integrations, Lead Docket isn't specifically designed for complex multi-touch attribution scenarios, and from my experience, it typically doesn't produce significantly improved results.

KNOW WHAT TO TRACK

It's essential to recognize there is such a thing as tracking too much. We frequently see firms collecting extensive data without spending adequate time analyzing or acting on it. To avoid information overload, identify a clear set of meaningful KPIs and track them consistently. We'll go deeper into specific KPIs in the next chapter.

SYSTEM ATTRIBUTION VS. SELF-ATTRIBUTION

An important distinction to understand is between "system attribution" and "self-attribution":

- **System Attribution:** This is data automatically captured by your tracking tools (like Google Ads or CallRail). It's reliable and unbiased. But it may not be always available since some leads will come in through non-tracked channels.
- **Self-Attribution:** This is information gathered when you directly ask leads how they heard about you. Although less precise—clients might incorrectly recall seeing your ad somewhere you haven't advertised—it's still valuable because it illustrates their *perception* of what brought them to call you. Some would argue that this is even more important than the actual channel or button they clicked.

If you find self-attribution data useful, create a dedicated field in Lead Docket to consistently gather this information.

Pro tip: Here's a useful sales psychology tip from the book *Influence* by Robert Cialdini: instead of asking "Where did you hear about us?" try asking, "Who should we thank for referring you to us?" This subtly signals to leads that you have a trusted referral network and reinforces their confidence in choosing your firm.

CLOSING THE MARKETING LOOP WITH A FEEDBACK LOOP

After properly tracking and attributing your leads, there's one more step: closing the loop with your marketing vendors. Marketing vendors typically only see initial actions (like clicks or calls) and rarely have visibility into your actual signed cases. Vendors might report giving you one hundred leads, but without seeing how many turned into signed cases, they can't effectively optimize their campaigns.

That's why we recommend setting up a "feedback loop,"

where you send information about signed cases back to your vendors. Lead Docket supports this through webhook integrations. To implement this, ask your vendors for an endpoint URL to push data automatically. Not all vendors can handle this directly, so you may need to use scheduled reports instead—but either way, establishing this feedback loop is valuable for your marketing optimization. Be careful if the vendor asks you for your application program interface (API) key. We'll explain this in more detail in the integration chapter, but treat that key with extreme care! Whoever has it can access every single piece of information in your Lead Docket.

Pro tip: Few marketing vendors suggest this, but consider requesting they set up Google Offline Conversions or Facebook Conversions (which are a recent addition). This tool allows you to send Google detailed information about the leads you signed, enabling Google's algorithms to optimize for true conversions rather than just clicks or calls. You'll typically need middleware like Zapier to connect Lead Docket data to Google offline conversions.

Chapter 02.03

Choose What to Track

Now let's pinpoint exactly what to do with the data you've gathered. It's crucial to have a clear process for analyzing your data, whether through weekly reports generated directly from Lead Docket or through dashboards and visualization tools reviewed daily. Different operational scales might require different tools, but the principle remains the same: ignoring your collected data means you're wasting valuable resources.

Remember, law firms today are essentially data-driven businesses. Leveraging insights from your data is not merely optional; it's essential for staying competitive in the modern market.

Here are some recommended KPIs to focus on—this list isn't exhaustive, but it highlights key metrics that provide actionable insights.

Suggested metrics to track:

- **Conversion Rate:** Track week-over-week and analyze performance by individual team members.
- **Cost per Lead, Cost per Wanted Lead, and Cost per Signed Case:** Monitor these month-over-month, as tracking trends over time is crucial for spotting meaningful patterns.
- **Breakdown by Campaign or Medium (Google, Facebook, etc.):** Evaluate each marketing channel's effectiveness to understand what's working and what's not.
- **Overall Growth Rate for Your Practice:** Measure this to gauge long-term marketing effectiveness and overall firm health.

Bonus metric:

- **ROI by Marketing Source:** Though valuable, keep in mind this metric has some caveats. ROI calculations can vary based on numerous factors, so interpret these results carefully and in context.

A NOTE ON ROI CALCULATIONS

ROI (return on investment) might seem like a buzz word metric, and it is in fact helpful for measuring marketing success. However, realistically calculating ROI is much more complex than it initially appears. At its simplest, ROI involves calculating your cost per case and dividing it by your average case value. For example, if you spend $1,000 in marketing to acquire one case and that case generates $10,000 in attorney fees, your ROI is 10:1. While this concept seems straightforward, accurately determining the revenue generated from a case can be challenging. Factors complicating ROI include long settlement cycles and multiple small payments spread over the life of a case.

Another significant consideration is the timing of these metrics. If you calculate your cost per case today or this month, which average case value should you use: how much you made this month, or how much you will eventually make when today's cases settle (which could be months or even years from now)? True ROI can only be fully understood over extended periods, making it difficult to rely solely on short-term ROI calculations.

My recommendation is this: get a precise grasp of your cost per case, as this is entirely achievable within Lead Docket. Separately, work closely with your Filevine or case management team to determine an average case value for each practice area. While there might be differences between litigation and pre-litigation cases, a sufficiently large sample size will give you a reliable average. Use this average case value combined with your cost per case as an approximation of your ROI. However, don't get overly fixated on ROI alone. For practical and immediate decision-making regarding intake and marketing effectiveness, your best metric is typically your cost per case.

Chapter 02.04

Tracking Your Marketing Expenses

Only a few firms truly take advantage of a valuable feature in Lead Docket: tracking marketing expenses. You should be among them. Lead Docket enables you to enter and monitor how much you spend on each individual marketing source by navigating to Manage > Expenses.

This feature allows you to clearly track major marketing expenses such as Google Ads, television, and Facebook Ads, separately. More importantly, it provides an accurate overall cost per case, consolidating all your marketing sources and leads in one place.

We highly recommend inputting these expenses monthly. This can easily be done using a template spreadsheet and typically involves no more than a dozen categories—consider your main marketing expenditures, such as billboards, television ads, Google Ads, SEO, and miscellaneous expenses. Once these figures are compiled into a spreadsheet, simply import them into Lead Docket each month.

While automated integrations might seem appealing—such as directly connecting QuickBooks to Lead Docket—our experience indicates this approach often results in messy and less actionable data. For most firms, a manual monthly import takes around fifteen minutes and provides clear, reliable insights.

Here's a link to a video walking through how to do it.

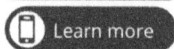

How to Add Expenses via Spreadsheet—seven minutes

Chapter 02.05

Tips to Better Convert and Retain Leads

PRACTICAL MARKETING TACTICS TO MOVE THE NEEDLE

This subchapter can genuinely improve your marketing results. If you don't implement anything else from the previous sections, at least pick one item from this list. These are practical and tested marketing strategies that work.

01—SEND A THANK-YOU MESSAGE WITH YOUR CONTACT CARD

Many firms don't realize that Lead Docket allows you to instantly message any new opportunity with attachments. We recommend sending a brief thank-you message and attaching your firm's contact card. You might say something like:

> Thank you for contacting us! Someone from our team will reach out shortly. To ensure you don't miss our call, please add our contact card to your phone. Thank you, [Your Firm's Name].

This small step improves your initial call success and greatly enhances the effectiveness of your follow-up efforts (Chase). If a lead has your contact saved, they're more likely to answer subsequent calls.

Pro tip: Some services allow you to send a link that automatically opens the user's "Add Contact" page on their phone. Look into these tools to streamline this even further.

02—ASK FOR GOOGLE REVIEWS AT INTAKE

This might seem counterintuitive at first—firms typically ask for reviews at the end of a case—but we've seen firms significantly boost their Google reviews by asking for them immediately after a successful intake call. If your intake team is trained well and makes the client feel genuinely heard, they can say something friendly like:

> Mr. John, if you appreciated my assistance today, it would really help me if you could leave us a quick Google review mentioning my name. My boss would love to see it, and so would I! I'll send you a quick link—it'll only take thirty seconds.

Some firms even incentivize intake staff or promise charitable donations for each review, which adds extra motivation.

Be mindful that this strategy has a downside. Clients may get hyperaware of your care for Google Reviews, so if you do disappoint them in the end, they may know to go to Google and leave you a bad review there. In my experience, the reward of many five-star reviews far outweighs the risk. Plus, you should not be disappointing the client in the first place. (Read the part about customer satisfaction reviews to create a safety net around client experience.)

03—AUTOMATE YOUR INITIAL FOLLOW-UP

We'll discuss automation in more detail later, but Lead Docket allows you to automatically respond to leads with follow-up questions. This works especially well in highly competitive case types, ensuring your leads remain engaged with your firm instead of immediately shopping around.

04—ALLOW LEADS TO SCHEDULE THEIR OWN APPOINTMENTS

Lead Docket integrates natively with Calendly, enabling leads to book appointments directly from your messages. The lead is automatically moved to the "Scheduled" status, and appointments appear on your or your attorney's calendar seamlessly. Be sure to leverage this feature to streamline your scheduling. The simple act of giving the lead a way to engage directly on their own terms can be very effective.

05—CUSTOMIZE YOUR CHASE MESSAGES

Your choice of wording in follow-up (Chase) messages can significantly impact response rates. We recommend regularly testing different versions of your messages. By monitoring your reports, you can quickly determine which messages are most effective.

06—SURVEY YOUR LOST LEADS

Using simple tools like Formstack or Jotform combined with Zapier, you can inexpensively survey leads you've lost. This gives you two important insights:

- Valuable feedback on why leads were lost, helping improve your intake process.
- Occasionally, another chance to convert a lost lead.

One firm we worked with achieved a 10 percent response rate, gaining important insights and recapturing leads regularly. More on this in one of our case studies further down.

ANALYZE YOUR OFFLINE MARKETING EFFORTS

Traditional advertising (e.g., TV ads) can be tough to track accurately. While unique phone numbers for each ad or station help somewhat, many viewers still find you through online searches later. But don't get stuck on perfect attribution—instead, focus on trends. For instance, if your dedicated TV ad number generates ten calls one month and thirty calls the next (after changing stations or messaging), these changes indicate something valuable. Monitor trends consistently, and feel free to test new approaches regularly.

Chapter 02.06

Optimizing Intake with Lead Docket

One of Lead Docket's most powerful features is its intake work-flow, which includes automated tasks and messages triggered by status changes. Think of Lead Docket's intake as an assembly line with several conveyor belts, each representing a different lead status. Your intake team's primary responsibility is to determine the appropriate status—or conveyor belt—for each lead. Once placed correctly, Lead Docket automatically sends out messages and assigns tasks, ensuring no leads slip through the cracks. This feature sets Lead Docket apart from many other CRMs and can significantly streamline the workload for your intake specialists.

Optimizing your intake process involves several key com-ponents, but first, it's essential to thoroughly understand your intake workflow. If you've been using Lead Docket for some time, we encourage you to visit your Intake Dashboard tab and closely examine each status box on the right-hand side of the screen. Each box represents an active status in your intake pipeline.

Pay particular attention to potential pipeline issues. For

example, if your "Pending Sign-up" status box shows dozens or even hundreds of leads that have been sitting idle for weeks or months (trust us, we've seen this happen), it clearly indicates a workflow problem. The intake person may even have a good reason for it, but this means the status isn't properly configured, or your intake team doesn't understand when to move leads forward.

We highly recommend creating a simple "cheat sheet" that describes each status in Lead Docket, detailing exactly when a lead should be placed into a specific status, when they should be moved out, and how often to follow up with them. This document forms the backbone of your intake workflow. If you're working with an optimization consultant, ensure they're familiar with this document and your overall process.

Addressing and clearing bottlenecks in your intake pipeline and consistently following up on leads may not be flashy, but it is effective. Roll up your sleeves, tackle the details, and you'll quickly see improvements in your intake efficiency and overall results.

THE INTAKE DASHBOARD SCREEN

I'll let Eric Coffman, Founder of Lead Docket, maybe the person who has seen the most number of Lead Dockets out there, chime in here:

> Of note, one of the more common situations I see with a messy dashboard is lack of decision-making or lack of authority to make a decision.

> Firms get a lead that they aren't sure they want. No one decides, so that lead stays in Assigned for months on end with no action.

The intake team has to look at that lead every single time they view the dashboard, and over time, the Intake Dashboard, which is supposed to be hot active leads, becomes a dumping ground for undecided leads that certainly have already moved on.

There are two solves for this:

- Task templates to ensure these leads have follow-up steps.
- MAKE A DECISION. Strive not to let a lead sit in a single status for more than one business day. If you want it, pursue it. If you don't, reject it. Don't let it sit undecided.

Well said, Eric.

REFERRALS IN LEAD DOCKET

Referrals in Lead Docket deserve special attention. In fact, Lead Docket is widely known for its robust referral dashboard and capabilities. If your firm refers out cases, you do not want to leave money on the table—actively track these referrals to ensure you receive your fees.

Lead Docket comes equipped with a dedicated "Referred Out" status, complete with a practical set of substatuses designed to manage most referral scenarios effectively. The general concept is straightforward: once a lead is marked as "Referred Out," you have two primary options:

- **No Follow-Up:** Use this substatus when you're referring out leads without expecting a referral fee, so tracking their acceptance isn't necessary.
- **Pending Review:** Choose this substatus if you need to actively track the referral. Selecting this status automati-

cally triggers a message to your referral partner, prompting them to review and accept the lead. From this point, you can effectively monitor the referral to ensure you don't lose sight of potential income.

This feature can benefit significantly from visual walk-throughs and examples. Here is a helpful video that explains how to maximize Lead Docket's referral tracking features.

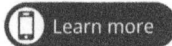

Referral Dashboard Overview—twelve minutes

Chapter 02.07

Message Templates (and Snippets)

This chapter partially overlaps with an earlier chapter about message templates. If you haven't yet reviewed it, please refer back to Chapter 01.08 for an overview and setup instructions.

For optimization, the next step is to elevate your message templates. My primary recommendation is to narrow your criteria and highly customize your messages. For instance, consider creating distinct wording and messaging frequency for your highest-value leads (e.g., five-star or million-dollar cases). The customization possibilities are extensive, particularly if your intake volume isn't extremely high. This is a scenario where smaller firms have an advantage!

Unfortunately, customization can become challenging as your firm grows. Many large firms we have worked with find it difficult to maintain highly customized messaging due to operational complexities. Managing multiple customized message paths might not be practical for firms with thousands of monthly leads. Therefore, if your firm isn't yet at such a scale, seize the opportunity to implement highly customized messaging while you can.

Additionally, don't underestimate the value of including links and attachments in your templates (Vcards for example—just don't overdo it with large images, or the phone carriers may mark your messages as spam). Small adjustments can often be manually tweaked to fit specific scenarios, further enhancing their effectiveness.

Pro-tip: Use Message Snippets! They are extremely helpful for your intake agents. Just set up a few snippets, and your intake specialists will thank you and ask for more.

Chapter 02.08

Task Management

Similar to the previous chapter, we've covered tasks extensively during the implementation section. If you haven't already reviewed it, I recommend referring back to Chapter 01.09 to fully understand tasks and their best practices.

When optimizing tasks, think of them as precise, actionable steps your intake team can take to significantly impact results. Be cautious about overusing tasks. If you or your team begin ignoring tasks regularly, that's a sign your task system isn't set up effectively. Tasks should always be relevant, helpful, and actionable. Rather than simply viewing tasks as a micromanagement tool, approach them from your intake specialist's perspective. Well-designed tasks serve as clear guidance, helping your intake team perform their roles more efficiently. Properly set tasks are typically welcomed and appreciated by your staff.

Risk Management

Chapter 02.09

Automation Rules

Automation Rules are an add-on feature for Lead Docket and are typically sold separately—you can request a quote directly from your Filevine representative. They're usually quite affordable and can be extremely valuable once enabled. After activation, you'll find a new tab under the "Manage" section in Lead Docket.

Automation Rules can streamline several critical tasks, allowing you to:

- Automatically move leads between statuses based on elapsed time or specific actions.
- Trigger certain workflows based on how questions are answered by the leads.
- Automatically send electronic signature documents.
- Directly post leads into Filevine.

Even if your intake volume isn't high enough yet to fully benefit from Automation Rules, it's helpful to be aware of this feature as you grow and look to boost efficiency.

Here are a couple of practical use cases we've seen work effectively:

QUALIFYING LEADS AND SENDING CONTRACTS AUTOMATICALLY

You can configure Automation Rules to immediately respond to website inquiries with a follow-up form containing a few critical questions. For example, when someone fills out a contact form on your website, they instantly receive a text message containing a link asking them to answer three or four essential qualifying questions. Once the answers are submitted, Lead Docket's automation can evaluate these responses and, if they meet your criteria, automatically send out a contract for electronic signature. After receiving the signed contract, Lead Docket can further automate what happens next in the workflow. This method is particularly powerful for highly competitive case types, ensuring rapid response and higher conversion rates.

Pro tip: Include a question on your intake form such as "Has it been more than ninety days since your accident?" This can protect your firm from inadvertently accepting cases that are close to or beyond the statute of limitations (SOL).

Chapter 02.10

Hidden Features You May Not Know About

Here are some lesser-known features in Lead Docket that can be quite powerful, depending on your processes and workflow.

CALL FUNCTIONALITY

Did you know you can make calls directly from Lead Docket? When the call functionality is enabled, an arrow icon will appear next to each lead's phone number. Clicking this icon initiates a call directly through Lead Docket.

Here's how it works: Lead Docket isn't a phone system itself. Instead, it calls your intake agent first using the number associated with their user profile. After the intake agent picks up, Lead Docket then connects the call to the lead.

This method has several benefits:

- **Consistency:** The lead receives calls from the same number they receive texts from, making communication clear and trustworthy.
- **Call Logging:** Calls made through Lead Docket are automatically logged under the "Calls" tab within each lead's profile. This provides a valuable record of all contact attempts. (If you are thinking, "Wait, I don't see a 'Calls' tab in my lead docket," then you don't have it enabled.)

However, there's one potential downside: if your phone system reports call data, these calls will all show up as originating from Lead Docket, potentially affecting your call reporting.

LEAD FORMS

Lead Forms are subsets of your intake questions that you can send via text or email for the lead to answer at their convenience. You can customize these questions, and responses automatically integrate back into Lead Docket. You can send these manually or set them to trigger automatically based on certain statuses using Automation Rules.

This feature streamlines intake by allowing you to gather detailed information without prolonging initial phone calls. For example, your intake team doesn't need to spend valuable call time gathering insurance details; instead, they can simply send a link, allowing the lead to fill in details at their own pace.

STATUS REQUIRED FIELDS

One of our favorite Lead Docket features is the ability to require specific fields based on lead status, ensuring data integrity for accurate reporting.

You might initially set fields like "address" as mandatory, which can frustrate intake teams dealing with leads who aren't ready to provide this information yet. To avoid this issue, Lead Docket allows fields to be required only for specific statuses. A common and practical example is making the address required only once a lead has officially signed up—at that point, the intake specialist should realistically have that information.

The "address" example is common, but you can apply this approach to other custom fields to improve reporting accuracy significantly. To understand the importance, try running a report on the gender of your signed leads; you might be surprised by how many are marked "unknown." Setting gender as a required field only at the "Signed Up" stage would immediately solve this issue.

Chapter 02.11

Managing Your Intake Team

When it comes to managing your intake team, Lead Docket provides several valuable features to make the process smoother and more effective. The approach you use for managing a small intake team of two people will likely differ significantly from the approach needed for managing a larger team of 120 intake specialists. However, we've seen firms successfully manage both scenarios using Lead Docket—it's just a matter of adapting the available tools to fit your team's size and specific workflow.

The fundamental principles for managing your intake team are similar to managing your marketing efforts: clearly define the metrics you'll track and select KPIs that meaningfully drive desired behaviors. In general, I favor tracking outcome-based metrics rather than task-oriented metrics. Tracking outcomes means evaluating the final results and giving your team the autonomy to decide what tasks they perform to achieve those results. Another valid approach is tracking specific tasks, but only if you're absolutely certain those tasks consistently drive your desired outcomes.

Both of these management strategies have merit, and their effectiveness will largely depend on your team's characteristics and operational needs. Some intake teams benefit greatly from clear, specific tasks—even though this can sometimes feel like micromanagement if not handled carefully—while others excel when allowed more ownership over their processes. The key is to recognize that task-level management should only be employed if you're completely confident those tasks reliably produce successful outcomes, and by "completely confident," I mean based on evidence and data—not just a gut feeling.

Lead Docket supports both management styles by providing excellent visibility into your team's performance through various KPIs. Let's start with outcome-based tracking.

OUTCOME METRICS

Conversion Rate: In my opinion, conversion rate is the single most important KPI for managing an intake team. It measures the percentage of your "wanted" leads that you successfully convert into signed cases. This KPI is widely used in sales management because it directly reflects your intake team's effectiveness.

To accurately measure your conversion rates, it's crucial to ensure Lead Docket correctly defines what a "wanted" lead is. By default, Lead Docket considers any lead that isn't explicitly rejected or referred out as a wanted lead. However, custom statuses in Lead Docket allow you to precisely refine this categorization. Remember, this "wanted" designation is dynamic and changes as leads move through your intake pipeline.

Occasionally, firms ask to add a custom field asking if a lead is "qualified" with a simple yes/no response. I strongly advise against this approach because Lead Docket already has a robust built-in method to handle this categorization. Typically, problems arise only when firms misunderstand how Lead Docket determines a "wanted" lead. To avoid confusion, review your status definitions under the "Manage" tab to make sure your statuses accurately reflect the leads you consider wanted. (You can even define this at a granular substatus level.)

Another frequent discussion is whether leads in the "Chase" status—those who have not yet been fully qualified or contacted—should count as wanted leads. There isn't a universally correct answer here. Some firms choose not to include uncontacted Chase leads in their wanted lead count, while others separate Chase leads into "Chase-qualified" and "Chase-no contact," clearly indicating which leads have been contacted and deemed desirable versus those that haven't been reached yet. This approach often yields more precise insights.

Additionally, you must define how to categorize leads that stop responding: do you label them as "lost" or "rejected"? Misclassifying nonresponsive leads as rejected prematurely can artificially inflate your conversion rate. A practical guideline is to ask, "Who ended the conversation?" If your firm decided not to pursue a lead, it's "rejected." If the lead stops responding or "ghosts" you, it's typically considered "lost."

I strongly encourage you to be strict and realistic with your KPIs. Intake managers and firm leaders often subconsciously aim to make their numbers look better by setting overly generous standards so they can have a "95 percent" conversion rate and feel aligned with what "experts" are saying at conferences.

While appealing in the short term, this ultimately harms both the team's growth and the firm's overall success. Setting realistic and challenging KPIs motivates continuous improvement. Teams with a clear goal and determination to reach it find creative and innovative ways to improve performance—ways you might never have thought of yourself.

You can easily monitor your conversion rates in Lead Docket by navigating to Reports > Statistics by Role.

TASK MANAGEMENT

Lead Docket also excels in task management, allowing you to keep close tabs on your team's actions. First, revisit earlier chapters to ensure your tasks are clearly defined and meaningful. Once tasks are properly set up, Lead Docket provides visibility into completion rates and overdue tasks, helping you verify that your team performs all necessary actions.

You can also assign manual tasks directly as you review individual leads and identify specific follow-up actions needed. While achieving perfect task management is challenging, Lead Docket equips you with all the necessary tools to significantly improve your team's productivity and accountability.

One caveat is that at the time of writing, Lead Docket doesn't have comprehensive reporting for tasks, so keep that in mind as you design your methodology.

Chapter 02.12

Lead Docket's AI Features

Lead Docket's AI features are among its newest and most exciting additions, focusing primarily on two key areas: summarization and prediction.

SUMMARIZATION

The summarization functionality in Lead Docket includes three main options:

- **Lead Summary:** This powerful feature generates a concise paragraph summarizing all intake questions answered by the lead. It compiles the details provided during the intake process into a clear and readable format, significantly simplifying your initial review.
- **Message Summarization:** You can summarize all messages related to a lead, capturing the overall tone and key topics from extended conversations found in the Messages tab.

- **Notes Summarization:** This option condenses notes from the lead's record into an easily digestible summary, although it tends to be less frequently utilized compared to the lead summary.

In my experience, the lead summary is the most beneficial and widely used summarization feature. It allows attorneys and intake specialists to quickly grasp essential case details. For example, the lead summary can be shared with attorneys or potential referral partners, enabling them to quickly decide whether a case warrants further review or action. More on this in a case study from the Law Brothers further in the book.

FEE PREDICTION

The Fee Prediction feature leverages machine learning developed by Lead Docket's team. It evaluates various responses provided during intake to estimate how likely a lead is to result in a fee. Our observations indicate it is consistently accurate, making it a valuable tool for intake teams to efficiently assess lead potential.

Some practical applications of the Fee Prediction feature include:

- **Auditing Rejected Leads:** Review your rejected leads to identify any marked as highly likely to generate fees. This practice can highlight potentially valuable leads that might have been prematurely dismissed.
- **Improving Intake Decisions:** Using the prediction score, your intake team can prioritize or further investigate leads predicted to be valuable, ensuring you don't overlook promising cases.

ADDITIONAL USES AND RECOMMENDATIONS

We've seen these AI-driven features positively impact several firms. If you haven't explored them yet, we strongly recommend trying them out. At the very least, being aware of these capabilities is beneficial as you continue optimizing your intake processes.

Chapter 02.13

Lead Docket Payments

Lead Docket Payments is a particularly helpful feature for firms that do not operate on contingency fees. Practices specializing in family, immigration, or criminal law or any firm using time-based billing can significantly benefit from the convenience of sending payment requests directly from within Lead Docket. The payment requests are easy to generate and send, requiring only a few clicks. Additionally, if your firm already utilizes File-vine Payments, you'll experience seamless integration between the two systems.

In our Case Study 02 later, you'll see a real-life example of an immigration firm who took Lead Docket Payments to the next level.

If you'd like to explore this feature further, we'll cover payments in greater detail in the video linked below.

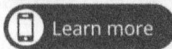

Lead Docket Payments—three minutes

Chapter 03

Reporting from Lead Docket

Reporting in Lead Docket has long been a favorite topic of mine, especially as I've pioneered Lead Docket dashboards for multiple firms. What fascinates me most is how running a Lead Docket system creates a treasure trove of data that very few firms fully leverage. Here are some key aspects to understand about Lead Docket reporting, progressing from basic to advanced.

STARTING WITH THE BASICS

Lead Docket comes equipped with several built-in reports that are great for quick, actionable insights. I've discussed many of these reports extensively in YouTube videos and webinars, but for this chapter, I'll highlight one of my favorites: the **Leads Over Time** report.

When you open the Leads Over Time report, you'll see three distinct lines representing your leads, wanted leads, and signed-up cases across a specified timeframe. Personally, I prefer to view this report week-over-week rather than daily to smooth out daily fluctuations and better understand overall trends:

- The top line represents your total leads.
- The middle line shows your wanted leads.
- The bottom line reflects your signed-up leads.

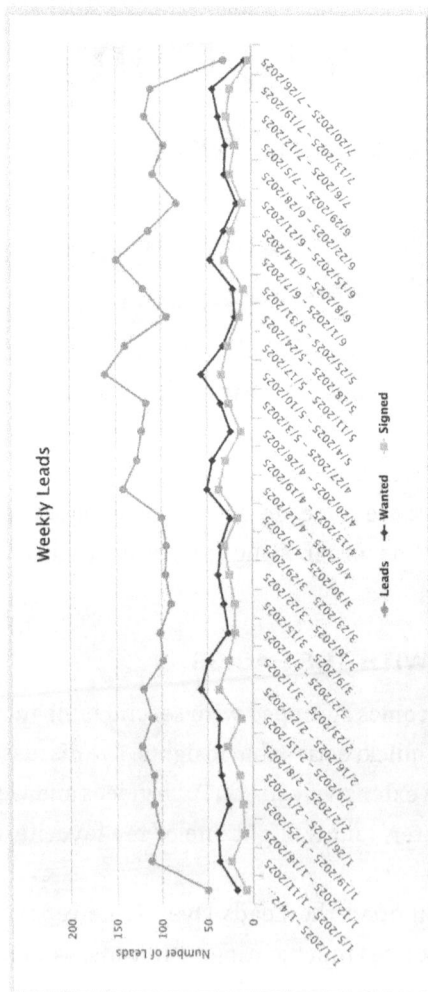

With a quick glance, this visual gives you a clear understanding of trends. Are your leads trending upwards, but your wanted leads aren't keeping pace? That might indicate your marketing is generating leads, but they're not well-qualified. If your wanted leads are increasing but signed-up leads aren't following suit, this may point to a conversion issue within your intake team.

In short, these three lines—and the gaps between them—can provide significant insights at a glance.

Here are some other resources about built-in reports in Lead Docket.

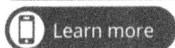

INTERMEDIATE REPORTING: EXPORTING DATA TO SPREADSHEETS

After making full use of Lead Docket's built-in reports, the next level is exporting your data to Excel or Google Sheets for more advanced analysis. Using spreadsheets allows you to harness greater analytical capabilities to dive deeper into your data.

A good example is analyzing your conversion rate over time. I would argue that reviewing your conversion rate for only this week or this month doesn't provide enough context. You should evaluate conversion rates month-over-month or week-over-week for at least the past year to see if your performance is improving or declining. Sometimes, trends over time are more telling than the actual numbers themselves. Same for Cost per Lead values.

To accomplish this, you can export data from Lead Docket using the Leads Report and then use Excel or Google Sheets to manipulate the data and calculate meaningful metrics.

As we are writing this book, Lead Docket is just releasing a new Leads Report with enhanced capabilities around column selection and filtering, making this a much more powerful tool.

We'll keep this as a QR code that you can scan to get more details since this feature will likely change significantly in the near future.

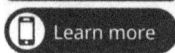

Pro tip: You can schedule these customized reports to be sent to you regularly. Additionally, if you're skilled with Excel, you can even automate these reports and their calculations using macros, saving time and ensuring consistent analysis.

ADVANCED REPORTING: AUTOMATED DASHBOARDS AND DATA SCIENCE

The highest level of Lead Docket reporting involves systematically extracting your data into an external database to create automated, real-time dashboards. These dashboards can handle complex calculations and can even send alerts based on KPI variations. This is where data science comes into play, elevating your intake management significantly.

I've built multiple advanced reporting solutions and hundreds of customized dashboards designed to help firms leverage their data effectively. The insights derived from these dashboards have been fascinating and transformative for many firms. Unfortunately, most of these are proprietary information that cannot be shared. One of our clients shared a fascinating part of our dashboards in this webinar if you would like to see more:

However, I encourage you to first master the basic and intermediate reporting techniques described above before moving onto advanced reporting solutions. Jumping directly into advanced dashboards without an understanding of your data and clearly defined KPIs often leads to frustration, both for you and the data analyst (like me) building these solutions. Take the process step-by-step, and you'll find advanced reporting much more rewarding and effective.

Chapter 04

Integrating Lead Docket via Zapier

If you haven't heard about Zapier, you're in for a treat. Zapier is what's known as a "no-code" automation platform, sometimes called a middleware—a software that connects two different software systems without requiring coding knowledge or complex development skills.

Lead Docket is specifically designed to integrate seamlessly with such automation platforms because it supports webhooks and has an open API. By incorporating Zapier, you significantly expand what Lead Docket can achieve, opening doors to virtually limitless automation possibilities. Speaking from experience, I've built integrations using Zapier that even surprised me with their capabilities—that's the true power of an open-API platform like Lead Docket.

WEBHOOKS AND API EXPLAINED
(IN SIMPLE TERMS)

Let's clarify these technical terms so you're well-informed:

- **Webhooks:** Think of webhooks as automatic messages or notifications sent between two software applications. They are triggered by specific events or actions. For example, when a new lead is created in Lead Docket, a webhook can automatically send this information to another system, such as a CRM or email marketing platform. Conversely, when other software sends data into Lead Docket through an "endpoint," a webhook receives this information and typically creates new opportunities or leads within Lead Docket. Although many firms casually refer to these incoming integrations as "API integrations," technically they are webhook-based integrations—though for practical purposes, the difference is minimal.

- **API:** An API provides structured access to the backend functionality of a software system, essentially allowing external programs or developers to interact programmatically with Lead Docket's data and operations. Under Manage > Settings, you'll find an API key and a link to the API portal (commonly called a Swagger page). With this API key, authorized users or developers can securely perform almost any action within Lead Docket, such as updating leads, changing statuses, or retrieving detailed reports. *Due to the extensive and sensitive nature of API access, you should never share your API key carelessly.* Providing your API key to a third-party vendor gives them unrestricted access to your Lead Docket data and operations. Always safeguard your API key diligently to ensure data security.

EXPANDING CAPABILITIES WITH ZAPIER

Without diving too deeply into the setup specifics, it's essential to recognize how significantly automation tools like Zapier or Workato can enhance Lead Docket's capabilities. However, it's equally important to approach this increased power responsibly. Keep in mind that complex automations typically lead to more complex processes, requiring ongoing maintenance and management.

SOME EXAMPLES OF AUTOMATIONS

Keep in mind as you read through these examples that they are custom built and often quite complex. If you like some of these ideas, feel free to reproduce them! Just please don't ask your Lead Docket admin person, "Can we have these automations done by Monday?"

- **Flagging manual errors:** You can set up Zapier to notify you or your team whenever someone makes certain mistakes in the data entry (marking a certain case type with the wrong office field, for example).
- **Asking for support:** You can add a button in your Lead Docket that gives your agent a way to ask for help on a certain lead.
- **Custom Chase messages:** We have taken this a step further and used AI to develop custom Chase messages to send to specific leads, customized to their specific case details.
- **Calculating SOL dates:** You can use a set of custom rules to calculate SOL dates based on incident dates.
- **Posting updates to Slack:** Integrate your leads activity with your Slack. Post five-star severity level leads to certain channels for example.

- **Sending documents to referral partners:** When posting a lead to a referral partner, if you wish to send documents as well you can.
- **Posting updates to your referral source:** You can automate updates from your Lead Docket or your Filevine to give your partners instant feedback on where the leads are.

The possibilities here are endless.

Chapter 05

Case Studies

As consultants, my team and I regularly partner with multiple law firms—sometimes even competitors of each other—which makes confidentiality and data privacy a cornerstone of our practice. At Vineskills, we take this responsibility seriously, carefully safeguarding client information and respecting intellectual property. With that in mind, special thanks go to the firms below, who generously agreed to share their experiences openly. Their real-life insights and stories will help you learn and grow, and we hope you find them valuable and engaging.

Case Study 01

Automations to Support Your Intake: Running a Large-Volume and High-Stakes Firm

(Arnold & Itkin Trial Lawyers)

In mid-2022, I began assisting Arnold & Itkin, a prominent plaintiff's firm founded in 2004 by attorneys Kurt Arnold and Jason Itkin. Their practice specializes in catastrophic personal injury and wrongful death cases—particularly maritime and offshore accidents, plant and refinery explosions, trucking incidents, and large-scale tort matters. Given their high-volume, high-stakes environment, flawless systems were essential.

When I joined, they were midway through a complex Lead Docket implementation and encountering several setbacks. With such large-scale projects, multiple factors extend beyond the basic software implementation, making every detail critical. We started methodically, first refining the intake questionnaire to align with their existing data and planned enhancements. Next, we carefully structured their statuses and tailored message templates to match the firm's distinct language and workflow.

Fast forward a few months and we did it! They went live, and their intake team successfully transitioned fully into Lead Docket. However, the journey didn't end there—our focus shifted to maintaining the system and pursuing ongoing enhancements.

Today, more than a year later, I continue working alongside their exceptional team. Their leadership is notably open-minded and committed to constant improvement, investing significant attention into keeping their systems highly effective. Consequently, their intake team now operates with remarkable accuracy, screening intricate cases efficiently, achieving both low error rates and strong conversions.

We implemented two specific improvements within Lead Docket:

ENHANCED INTAKE PRECISION

We built automations to assist the intake team with complex evaluations. One notable example calculates an estimated statute of limitations (SOL) date based on the incident date and several state-specific criteria. This automation provides intake agents with immediate clarity on case urgency, simplifying decision-making.

MASS TORT BATCH PROCESSING

Utilizing Lead Docket's open API, we streamlined handling mass tort cases. After migrating their legacy system, hundreds of cases needed to be accurately entered into both Lead Docket and Filevine. Instead of manual data entry, which was initially attempted, we quickly developed a Zapier-based automation that filled essential fields, assigned team members, and processed each lead in seconds. This approach drastically reduced the team's workload, freeing them to focus on higher-value tasks.

Case Study 02

Lead Docket for Immigration Firms

(Saavedra & Perez)
—Written by Shadae Pete

This chapter is written by Shadae Pete, Lead Docket optimizer and my colleague at Vineskills.

Another big practice area we see in Lead Docket more and more is immigration law. Founding attorneys Isabel Saavedra and Michelle Perez started their East-Coast-based immigration firm with a personal and passionate hand in the practice area. In their own words:

> We also understand how challenging the process of selecting an immigration attorney can be. During our own immigration processes, we worked with attorneys who didn't speak our language, didn't take the time to explain the process to us, and didn't make us a priority. That's why we have dedicated our lives to helping immigrants obtain and protect their right to be here.

This sentiment is evident not only in their client efforts and communication but even in the way they use and build their software systems.

As part of our work with Saavedra & Perez, we focused on two critical areas: the client intake and scheduling experience, and the automation and tracking for flexible payment options.

INTAKE & SCHEDULING ENHANCEMENTS

Using the built-in integration with Calendly in Lead Docket, we restructured the intake and scheduling process to ensure smoother client handling, better team coordination, and greater automation. With this integration, firms can schedule client consultations directly with attorneys and update the status in Lead Docket to track and text the client for these consultations. By using routing forms, clients can also be directed to the appropriate attorney, appointment length, and type of consult based on a series of questions. This worked well for the team—but there were still some minor frustrations that could not be done in the integration. By introducing Zapier, we were able to overcome some of these, such as providing reschedule links, canceling links, and bringing back valuable data into Lead Docket for more in-depth reporting on the types of appointments being scheduled. We were even able to work directly with the Lead Docket product team to update the native integration, finding that they could now include certain items like Zoom links in the appointment location to appear in outgoing client texts and emails.

FEES & EXPENSES AUTOMATION FOR REPORTING

As we mentioned before, Lead Docket has several built-in tools to track marketing spend and ROI. The key to using these tools is inputting both your expenses and client fees into the system. Traditionally, firms can add expenses one-by-one or import in bulk using a spreadsheet. With Saavedra & Perez, we took it a step further. Using Zapier, Google Sheets, and QuickBooks, we set up an automation that will automatically pull out expenses toward marketing spend and send them to an approvals sheet that links directly to Lead Docket. In addition to expenses, we need fees entered to accurately predict return. Unlike contingency-based firms, which involves a fee received at the end of a case's settlement, many immigration firms need a way to collect and track deposits and additional payments that will take place in the future. Saavedra & Perez, in particular, allows flexible payment options, including monthly payments that can extend over the year (or more in some cases). Lead Docket Payments is a built-in tool that allows users to seamlessly collect deposits and fees or send easy payment links to clients where they can pay on their end. Using Zapier (and some calculations), we implemented an automation that applies the appropriate deposit and future payments as needed for reporting once a client signs up. With these two automations, we hope to remove any manual efforts from tracking and reporting, all without interrupting the client or user experience.

Case Study 03

Customer Satisfaction Surveys

(Feller & Wendt)

In early 2024, while working closely with the Feller & Wendt team, it quickly became clear how client and staff satisfaction was embedded in the firm's identity, particularly due to the influence of Thaddeus Wendt and Matt Feller. They had long demonstrated genuine care and attention toward their employees and naturally extended this authentic approach to the firm's clients. After nearly two years of collaboration, it was evident that this emphasis on client satisfaction wasn't simply strategic—it was deeply aligned with their personal values and vision.

In the personal injury sector, client perception is particularly crucial because many significant cases come from referrals. It can literally mean millions of dollars. Understanding this, we started exploring ways to systematically and consistently collect feedback from clients at various stages of their journey with the firm. Even with robust procedures and well-defined guidelines,

I would argue that true success is measured by client satisfaction. Thaddeus recognized that prioritizing the client experience would have meaningful impacts both culturally and financially for the firm.

After months of careful testing and fine-tuning, we established an integrated client satisfaction system using Lead Docket and Filevine. This process included four specific points at which we gathered client feedback throughout each case, providing ongoing, valuable insights. Here's how we implemented it:

THE LOST SURVEY

If you only implement one suggestion from this case study, it should be the lost survey. It's a straightforward, effective method to gather valuable feedback and potentially recover leads that otherwise seemed lost. We set up a simple message template in Lead Docket, triggered whenever a lead entered the "Lost" status. This message typically said something like:

> We're sorry to see you go and would greatly appreciate understanding how we could have better served you. Please take a moment to answer a single question below.

This message included a link to a concise Jotform survey, where clients selected their reason for not proceeding or stopping communication from a dropdown menu. These responses were automatically logged back into Lead Docket and shared directly with intake managers and partners. Within days, we realized we had struck gold—the feedback was exceptionally helpful in improving intake experiences, and surprisingly, some previously unresponsive leads re-engaged, allowing us to recover potential cases without extra effort.

FILEVINE SURVEYS

Next, we expanded our feedback collection to capture satisfaction data throughout each case's lifecycle within Filevine. Although several third-party services offer automated messaging capabilities with Filevine, we found that Lead Docket's integration provided a seamless, in-house solution.

Using Lead Docket's native phase-mapping functionality, we triggered message templates based on specific phases within Filevine cases. Clients received a similar Jotform survey to complete, and the responses were automatically pushed back into Filevine through Zapier. These responses were organized into a dedicated customer satisfaction section, making them readily available for analysis and reporting through our business intelligence tools.

The solution proved to be both elegant and practical. We documented the entire process clearly, ensuring visibility and accessibility across all teams working in Filevine. Additionally, we developed comprehensive reporting dashboards in DOMO/Periscope, which calculated net promoter scores (NPS) at both the beginning and end of cases. This provided stakeholders with clear, continuous insights into the client experience being delivered by their team.

REFLECTIONS AND CULTURAL IMPACT

A few months after implementation, we noticed two significant and somewhat unexpected outcomes:

1. **Increased Survey Response Rates:** Response rates were unsurprisingly low. No one wants to respond to surveys. But we noticed that over time it actually improved, suggesting that paralegals and attorneys working in Filevine fully

embraced the importance of client satisfaction, leading to clients feeling more valued and consequently more willing to share their feedback.

2. **Rapid Spotting of Dissatisfaction:** By immediately alerting stakeholders whenever negative feedback was received, the team swiftly addressed client concerns, preventing escalation. Leadership fostered a supportive environment where all feedback—even critical—was welcomed openly and dealt with straight on, fostering a culture of continuous improvement and accountability.

Ultimately, the customer satisfaction surveys we implemented had positive implications far beyond simply gathering client feedback, positively influencing the firm's culture and approach to client service.

Case Study 04

Slack Referrals: Reshaping Referrals with Warm Transfers Using Slack

(The Law Brothers)

As all firm owners know, not all cases will be signed. With successful marketing, a law firm will end up with dozens, or hundreds, of leads that do not fit the criteria for the firm. These cases may fall outside their jurisdiction, apply to a different practice area, or may not meet your firm's specific intake criteria due to staffing or bandwidth considerations. The Law Brothers is a rapidly growing personal injury firm based in California, led by two visionary owners, Shervin and Shawn Lalezary. They recognized early on that their business model was built around providing focused, high-touch service—dedicating significant time, attention, and resources to every client they represent.

However, due to their extensive marketing across various channels, they were also receiving a high volume of inquiries involving practice areas outside their specialty or matters that they simply weren't equipped to manage. Rather than overlook these leads, they decided to monetize referrals and prioritize the client's experience when transferring cases.

Referrals are common in the personal injury industry, but the traditional approach of simply passing the client details to a referral firm—which might not always promptly follow up or effectively convert the lead—wasn't sufficient. The Law Brothers are community-driven—they want to ensure that even clients they refer to other businesses are still receiving immediate help. The Law Brothers envisioned a live referral network that would enable immediate, warm transfers of leads to their referral partners.

In partnership with the Law Brothers, we implemented a solution combining Lead Docket and Slack to achieve their goals. Leveraging their strong relationships with referral partners, the Law Brothers encouraged their network to use Slack for real-time referrals. This approach was notably straightforward because it attracted referral partners who were already tech-savvy or familiar with Slack.

By utilizing Lead Docket's webhooks and Zapier, intakers could instantly trigger a message to the selected Slack referral group with a simple prompt: "Are you interested in this lead?" Using a Slack integration tool called Polly, referral partners responded directly within Slack, and the first firm to click "Yes" would receive the lead immediately. The intake agent could then perform a seamless, warm transfer, enhancing the client's overall experience by demonstrating collaboration and genuine partnership between firms. The immediacy of this also helps encourage firms to stay connected and in-touch.

Several key factors contributed to the success of this automation:

- **AI-generated lead summaries:** Providing concise and relevant information enabled referral partners to quickly assess lead quality.
- **Inclusion of photos and documents:** Referral partners received additional context about the lead, facilitating informed decision-making.
- **Immediate automated matching:** Once a partner accepted a lead via Slack, automation within Lead Docket instantly assigned the lead to that partner and sent them additional details through message templates.

So what happens if everyone in the Slack group selects "No"? Thanks to the combination of tools (Zapier, Polly, Slack, and notably, Lead Docket's own native automations tool), this did not delay a decision on the lead. If everyone in the group selects no, it would trigger Lead Docket to send them to another desired group depending on their practice area.

After successfully testing this automation with a single case type, the Law Brothers expanded this model to multiple practice areas and states nationwide. Today, their referral network operates across various states, allowing them to significantly increase marketing spend, handle higher volumes of leads, and consistently provide a high-quality client experience.

It's worth noting that this Slack-based referral process serves as an entry point for a comprehensive and highly effective referral network. Considerable effort has gone into ensuring accurate case information sharing and tracking the progress of referrals among all partners—but exploring these deeper integrations might be best left to a future case study!

Case Study 05

How to Handle True High-Volume Intake

(Alexander Shunnarah Trial Attorneys)

When Mitri Shatara casually took to the stage at Lex Summit 2024 and put up their live Lead Docket system on the screen, the audience was left astounded. Most firms process leads by the dozens or maybe hundreds, but Alexander Shunnarah Trial Attorney handles them in thousands, representing one of the highest-volume Lead Docket instances anywhere.

Mitri's openness on stage highlighted not only their leadership's transparency but also their confidence in their processes. You might wonder how managing thousands of leads effectively is even possible, especially if you're feeling overwhelmed with just a few hundred. The secret is a finely tuned, deeply customized intake workflow. And some great leaders.

Working with Shunnarah's intake leaders, we took the time to understand their unique process—rather than just blindly applying general "best practices." (Quick note to other consultants reading this: don't simply recycle strategies from one firm to another. Real solutions require real understanding.)

Having collaborated extensively with the Shunnarah team, I believe one aspect is particularly critical to their high-precision, low-error intake process: the meticulous design of their intake questionnaire.

If you think your firm's questionnaire is robust, consider the complexity of the logic we developed for Shunnarah.

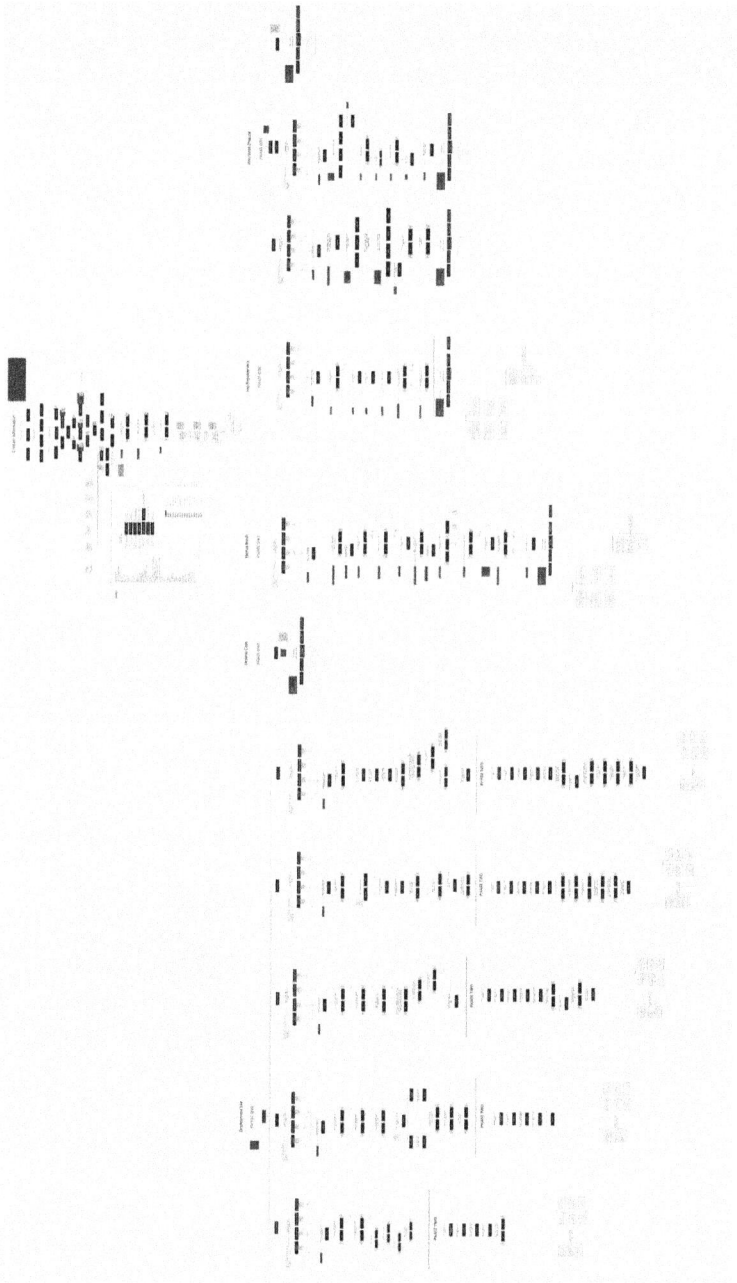

(We've included a screenshot—not for the proprietary details, of course, but just to illustrate the intricacy involved. And by the way, this screenshot is about one-fifth of the whole flowchart.)

Each case type has its own tailored flow, with every question guiding the intake agent logically to the next step. Hundreds of instructional texts further guide agents through these interactions, significantly minimizing potential errors.

Credit where it's due: Shunnarah's intake team, along with Shadae Pete from Vineskills, manage over a thousand constantly evolving custom fields with remarkable efficiency.

Another essential factor to Shunnarah's success is how thoroughly they manage incoming referral sources. Properly setting up integrations to track and provide automated feedback to referring partners demands extensive effort, but the returns are significant. Utilizing external partner IDs within webhooks, we enabled referral sources to push leads (alongside necessary documentation) directly into Lead Docket. Each lead is screened automatically, IDs are tracked seamlessly throughout the entire process, and data flows back into the referring partners' systems.

This precision allows Alexander Shunnarah Trial Lawyers to expertly handle an extraordinary volume of incoming referrals without missing a beat.

Chapter 06

Conclusion

If you've reached this point, you've likely recognized that managing Lead Docket is an ongoing process rather than a one-time task. Throughout this book, we've provided practical tools and approaches—from foundational setups to automation and advanced reporting—to help you get started.

While comprehensive, this book isn't intended to cover every detail. Instead, its purpose is to open your eyes to the many possibilities and opportunities Lead Docket offers. It serves as a starting point, encouraging you to explore further.

The real potential of Lead Docket comes from how thoughtfully you apply its features. The feature that one firm loves may not do much for another firm. So with each lead you process, each report you analyze, and each insight you gain, consider the effectiveness of your process and the impact of innovation.

Stay informed and curious about new features, enhancements, and integrations, considering how they can practically benefit your operations. This book is an offline medium, and Lead Docket is constantly improving, so stay tuned for its new releases.

Continuous improvement isn't about perfection; it's about regularly making your system better, one practical step at a time.

This book marks the beginning of your journey. Keep exploring, keep refining, and keep finding new ways to leverage all that Lead Docket can offer your firm.

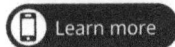

SCAN ME

Learn more